Pat's Poetry

Patricia Bramer Russell Richard

Copyright © 2016 Patricia Bramer Russell Richard

All rights reserved.

ISBN: 1540705617
ISBN-13: 978-1540705617

Dedication

What legacy can be left
To those for whom we care
My many lovely, happy memories
Are dancing everywhere…

Dedicated to my little women
Who brought joy I can't compare
For this and their growing up days
I have these lyrics to share…

Tomi, Lori, Amy & Julie

Contents

In Appreciation	i
Family	1
Fun With Pat	56
Friends	86
Seasons With Pat	109
Workdays	137
Holidays With Pat	151
Prayers	166
About the Author	184

In Appreciation

Pat's Poetry has been envisioned for many years and has been quite a journey. For anyone who desires to write poetry, I suggest you keep paper and pen close by. Make haste; thoughts come quickly and vanish in the same manner!

Many of my thoughts in rhyme have not been included on these pages. I am grateful for many who have crossed my path of life and for family and friends who have inspired me.

So, get comfortable and join me as I express my gratitude to those who have made this little book possible. I am grateful to my granddaughters, Hannah Barnes and Megan Dollarhide, and my son-in-law Pastor Doug and daughter Amy Shows for their time and support in organizing, editing, and making *Pat's Poetry* a reality. In addition, I thank my other three beautiful daughters: Tomi Yezak, Lori Lofton, and Julie Odle, and my ever-supportive and longtime friend, Shirley Adair, for years of love, encouragement, and prayers.

Finally, I praise my Maker and show appreciation for His inspiration.

Family

Patricia Bramer Russell Richard

A Prize

Dad and I have missed you, Tomi
While you've been gone away
And so we got you a little prize
That we hope is here to stay.

It can't be all used up
It should last for many years
It will be around for you to tell
Your secrets, joys and fears.

It's a tiny little thing now
And needs your love and care
But when the prize gets full grown
You will be its mistress, fair.

So love it and feed it
And to it fondly tend
We hope this little prize
Will become your best friend.

A Surprise for Tom

Saturday is my birthday
On August Seventeen
I don't know it yet, but
I'll be treated real keen.

Please come by to see me
And wish me many more
Between two and five
I'll greet you at the door.

It's not to be told –
Especially to me, that
I'll have a pretty cake
And coffee, punch or tea.

My birthday will be so happy
If you don't let me down
Come – and bring a smile
So I won't wear a frown.

Patricia Bramer Russell Richard

Alzheimer's

I look upon this happy face
As it smiles at me
A bit impish and filled with mischief –
This happy face I see

This man I view – no longer there
As I see his twinkling eye
Only memories past – are all that's left
My heart hurts and so I cry

Our Lord will take away our pain
And as our precious moments few
He'll bless us time and time again –
As I share these visits with you

Pat's Poetry

Amy (Beloved)

It's all too soon, Amy,
But the time is nearly here
Crockett days are almost over
The days forever dear.

Such a student of honor
With A's all the way
Recipient of two blue ribbons
For the starring one-act play.

Your love of the library
Is to read and keep abreast
Your help in the office
I know is best.

But the long hours of study
By being math accelerated
Has been a real challenge –
Now you're quite educated.

You play the flute well
And band is your pleasure
To sit in the first chair
Is also your treasure.

Of all our reminiscing
This one - let's repeat
Our very own best actress
Made junior high days complete.

I'm no poet, Amy,
But my thoughts are sincere
Dad and I are proud and pleased
God blessed us with you, dear.

Patricia Bramer Russell Richard

An Invitation for Lori

This is an invitation –
A party for all to share
There'll be country breakfast cooking
Don your jeans or western wear.

The wedding's just around the corner
Getting nearer by the hour
Please lend your help to fill the bags
So rice on us will shower

Now don't be late – come at ten
On Saturday, July thirty-one
We'll brunch and work and laugh
Come join in all the fun.

Announcement

There's going to be a wedding
And I will be the bride
And my sweetheart Charlie
Will be right at my side.

There won't be a big crowd
It's just a quiet affair
But we do have special friends
And with you we'd like to share.

So join in our good news
And enjoy our happiness
And wish us luck and fortune
Along with years of wedded bliss.

Please keep us in your thoughts
And say a prayer or two
That adjustments will run smooth
In this marriage so new.

A big date   Friday   2-14-92

April for Amy

April is a lovely month – though sometimes filled with showers
May brings weddings closer – and faster fly the hours.
June is proud of the time it holds
As sweethearts lives become one mold.

As vows are made to love and share
Remember then how much I care
How much I wish hope and happiness
And the peace of God's own tenderness.

At Day's End

This is for you – at day's end
You make my days fly by
So I can run home to
A very true blue guy.

He is very complimentary
He's full of love and kisses
He does all in his power
To fulfill all my wishes.

His arms are always open
He plays the game quite fair
Though sometimes he likes to tease me
I know he's always there.

I don't want to be unruffled
I want him to be my need
Our marriage is a blessing
A gift from God indeed.

Patricia Bramer Russell Richard

Bad Dream

She had such a bad dream
And woke with quite a start
That the thud could almost
Be heard from the racing of her heart!

We rushed to her rescue
Her Dad and I
And as she gave a scream
Our hearts gave a sigh.

But all she remembered as
She sat upright in her bed
Was that a "bunch of umbrellas"
Had fallen on her head.

Tho sorry for her disturbance
She said that they hurt
And as they fell so did she
Right down on her pillow quite curt.

Her eyes quickly closed tight
And so peaceful was she
I wondered just who had
A dream – my daughter, Tomi, or me!

Brother

My brother is such a great guy
He's just a boy at heart
So filled with jokes and humor
Making others laugh is his art.

Tho his body isn't well
Unless you saw him you'd not know it
My brother has lasting pain
His beautiful blue eyes show it.

He's not an old fellow – only 57
His back is bent, not straight anymore
His arms are bruised and hands are twisted
The frown on his brow shows pain to the core.

So special he is at accepting
The burdens that he's been dealt
You will love him and admire him
He will make your heart melt.

Patricia Bramer Russell Richard

<u>Brunch with Julie</u>

Please brunch with me at ten
On the twentieth of June
We'll have a bite to eat and then
You may leave by noon.

But your help I need
For an assembly line
To fill the bags with rice or seed
Don't leave me in a bind!

Charles Russell

Seven pounds and six ounces
And so quickly he came
A real lively bundle of joy
Crying and squirming
And Charlie is his name
A healthy and fine baby boy.

Brown hair and blue eyes
And such a tiny young thing
He watches intently at all
Soon he'll be running about
Love and laughter he'll bring
As we watch Charlie grow strong and tall.

Chelsy Anne

A lovely new grand daughter
Has come into our world
Her name is Chelsy Anne
And she's a darling little girl.

Her eyes are wide and bright
And as they gaze at us we see
She's wasting no time at all
Getting acquainted with you and me.

She's such a tiny bit of love
That has burst into bloom
And in our hearts she's creeping
Where there's lots and lots of room.

Keep her safe and healthy Lord
Under Your watchful care
Thank You for sending a beautiful daughter
For Lori and Eric to share.

Craig Thomas

Thank You Lord for Craig Thomas
With dark hair and eyes of blue
He seems to be so perfect
Made especially for us by You.

He's such a good baby
And already he's brought much delight
We stand and marvel at him
He is a beautiful sight.

Mother and Daddy are so very happy
Their hearts jump with joy
And Papaw and Oma are
Thrilled to have a grand boy!

Tho we know as he develops
There will be both laughter and tears
We thank you Lord for sending Craig
To add more love to our years.

Patricia Bramer Russell Richard

Crockett Class of '71

If you've just noticed the eighth graders grieving
It's because we're aware we soon will be leaving.

Crockett's been great in so many ways
And, for us, it's quite painful, these last few days.

We try to be cheerful and the happy year recall
But junior high days will be gone forever, in no time at all.

Remember next September when enthusiastic eighth graders arrive
That on school activities, this class also did thrive.

We know to grow strong in our great society
Our number one MUST is to behave with propriety.

As Freshmen next year, we'll be tops in our line
Just a good bunch of kids having just a good time.

We'll strive for good marks and remain quite select
For we are the BEST, and the "Best we'll reflect"

This is said not in jest, nor is it said jest for fun
We'll make Crockett proud, of our class of '71.

Daddy's Plea

"I wanted someone to talk to"
So often I heard this phrase.

But how I long to hear it again;
Right now and in future days.

"Call me up – spend a dime"
I didn't know there was limited time.

Only God knew, and God did care.
I know He answered Daddy's prayer.

His shaky walk, his wobbly cane –
I know Daddy feels no more pain.

Keep my Daddy close in sleep –
Take away these tears I weep.

For we are born to die, I know.
I just love my Daddy so.

You took him God, he's with you there.
He surely feels your loving care.

-Good-bye to my much loved Daddy-

Patricia Bramer Russell Richard

Doctor Amy

If it was what you wanted
I knew that do it you would
'Cause once you've made your mind up
You're like the "Little Engine that Could!"

In grammar and middle school
You set your goals so high
There were few challenges
That you let pass you by.

You received your diploma
With honors beside your peers
But this did not quench your desire
Of more knowledge for future years.

Off you went to college
Yes, you surpassed that too
When you received your Master's
We all were so proud of you.

Now that you're our doctor
We're bustin' at our seams
We're so very proud –
You've at last fulfilled your dreams.

Doug

Does your each new day begin anew

Or does every day show a certain view

Unaware you are so grand

Gracious and gentle – our preacher man

Erika Nicole

The little girl I remember
Would laugh and play and share
Her smile was big – her eyes so bright
She had curls in her hair
Full of life – this little one
With skin so soft, smooth and fair

The times she shared with me
After a day of school
Were happy and carefree
She never broke a rule
We bounced a ball – we ran a race
I could rarely keep her pace

We caught fuzzy worms
And in a cage they went
We picked their favorite nice green leaves
Soon lovely wings were sent
They grew and grew and grew
Then one day away they flew

I savor all these happy times
Time does not stand still
And as the joyful butterflies –
We too, must live God's will

For Julie at Aunt Babe's

Julie first was Tom's and mine

Until Amy came along

Lori came – our life did shine

I knew our home would fill with song.

Every heart was happy and gay

Russells together would work and play

Until several more years did pass and

Soon we had another lass.

She has filled our life with love.

Each child is a gift from above.

Love and happiness is wished Julie and Steve.

Long life and God's bless are my prayers.

Patricia Bramer Russell Richard

For Julie – Surprise Happy Birthday

Do you like surprises?
Well, there's one on the way
January thirty-first to be exact –
That's my eighteenth birthday!

Mom's having open house,
Please help me celebrate –
It's come and go or come and stay;
So don't fret about being late.

Please drop by to see me
And wish me many more –
Between five and nine,
I'll meet you at the door.

Your presence will be missed
My day will be so sad –
So do come by and stay a while
And make my birthday glad!

For Lori and Lonnie

Life is sweet –
It's also very short
To put yourself first means you're saving
The best for your sweetheart

Life is short –
Years have passed
To put yourself first means you're saving
Your best for the last

These frivolous thoughts and
Strange-seeming lines
Are filled with meaning
For your hearts from mine

Patricia Bramer Russell Richard

Happy Mother's Day to Mama

Today is Mother's Day
Our special day each year
There is love in my heart
Listen! And you'll hear.

I know you share my feelings
Mere words cannot express
The joy and laughter of children
Their warm tenderness.

Tho each Mother's Day, I'm one year older
Hope I'm given lots of time to watch my children
Grow and be blessed with a family
Sweet as mine.

I'm thankful for my motherhood –
Thankful for my mother, too
For I could not enjoy these things
If it had not been for you.

Howard

Howard is a man it's true

Of all the colors, he favors blue

Wouldn't you know he is quite wise

Always a twinkle in his eyes

Rarely does he make a fuss

Dependable and loves all of us

Jacob Michael

Just a tiny little baby boy

Always brings a lot of joy

Comes to us as a bright new toy

Often times grows much too fast

But the love we share will last and last!

Julie – Savor the Time

May into June
And love will bloom
After summer, follows fall
Then one day, you'll recall
How your life was spent
The blessings God lent
The days will seem to fly
You'll wonder where and why

Julie's Bosses

It's Bosses' Week,
Did you know?
If you did not,
I'm telling you so!!

Mom and Dad are my bosses at home
But here at school, I'm on my own.
When roll is called during first class hustle
No teacher calls for Julie Russell.

So Bosses Smith, Hellum, Bess, Horlacher, and Graves, too,
I've appreciated you ALL year through.
During first period I've given my best –
I've tried and I hope I've passed the test.

This is to say I think you all are fine.
And thanks for keeping me in line.
Now, we'll have no more fuss –
As Bosses, you all deserve A+

Life's Chapter

Tomi, listen to my message
It comes right from my heart
Some days are good; others great
Each one has a fresh start

Tho we all have bad days
When troubles seem to mount
That's when it's time to sit down
And all our blessings count

Life would be no challenge
If everything came with ease
And on those ordinary days
We're calm and full of peace

Unless, of course, we're restless
And searching for that conquest
That fills us with uncertainty
And overcomes us with anxiousness

But the Lord will soothe our being
Each time of life's a chapter
And our faith and trust in Him
Carries us today and each day after

Lonnie

Looking onward and forward

Only life filled with help and care

Never a lacking for a job well done

Never a dull moment – always time for fun

In being a good father and husband – a tribute to see

Every day for Lori and for his family

Lori – A Beach Bum

You will find her there
Her Lord to share
In Nature's beauty and flowers
A blazing sunset, a glowing moon
And even in the showers

His presence is alive and real
And this she cannot conceal
In her eyes it shows
Wherever she goes, her God
Is there through life's woes

A starfish she may find
A broken sand dollar left behind
A sea bean with its hamburger rind
As her collection grows and grows
The search keeps God always in her mind

Patricia Bramer Russell Richard

<u>Lori – Our Teacher</u>

A soft and inner beauty
Reflects the gentleness you hold
As you meet your task at hand
As today's lesson is told

Your voice is sure and precise
The method clear and firm
Your lesson plan detailed
For each child to learn

An unyielding tenacity you show
As you vow your goals to meet
The challenge to educate children
Is your pleasure and your feat.

Mama's Surprise

Will you share a secret
And promise not to tell
Just drop by and say hello
And wish my mother well
She's going to have a birthday –
Come – we'll celebrate
Circle your calendar so you
Won't forget the date
Just bring your love and laughter
And lend a little of your time
To make this day quite special
For this dear mother of mine.

Megan Dale

Lord, you've sent us a baby
So precious and new
You've lent her to us
To watch over for you

She has quite a good grip
And a healthy young wail
Tho something inside her
Still is quite frail

You are so just Lord
And so willing to share
As you place this sweet child
In our loving care

Please bless her and please
Lord soon make her well
We praise you and thank you
For sending Megan Dale.

Mumps

To my sweet daughter, Amy,
Who's all closed in
There's just one thing to keep up –
That's your chin.

I know you get lonesome
At home all alone,
But you can keep busy
This, you have shown.

So, remember, chin up!
Don't get down in the DUMPS
For this is what happens to kids
Who have the MUMPS

My Charlie

You've been good for me
You've helped my smile return
You are special to me
And for your company I yearn.

I like your smile –
The comfort of your touch.
To know that you care
Means so very much.

I like to see a movie with you,
To dance – and jitterbug.
I like to have dinner with you
And accept a warm and tender hug.

Friends have noticed that
I am happy and carefree.
I count on you
For my serendipity!

I thank the Lord
For sending you my way.
I pray He will bless and
Keep you well and safe each day.

My One Plus Four

I am blessed so very much
Nowhere else could I find
Four daughters nice and sweet –
A husband, good and kind.

Let me share my love with you
Through all our years
Together we'll spread sunshine
Through sadness and tears.

The desires of a mother
Can be selfish, it's true
I'm no exception – I wish
Only the best for each of you.

Try hard to be understanding
Be thoughtful and kind
If you search, in your lifetime
Much happiness you'll find.

God has given us this Mother's Day
I hope to share many more
Stay always close to me
I love you: My one plus four.

Patricia Bramer Russell Richard

My Perfect Grandkids

There's nothing quite like grandkids
To tickle your nose
To tug at your hair
And to catch wiggly toes

They stare at your eyes
They twist on your ear
They hold to your fingers
Before the age of one year

They're kinda like puppies
All cuddly and round
But if you should cross one
Out comes a loud sound

They pull on your skirts
And grab round your knees
They're clinging and hanging
Like rats after cheese

But my grandkids are perfect
And they have angel wings
They're beautiful and precious
And they make my heart sing

My Youngest Queen

There is a lovely young lady in my life
Generally she's filled with smiles – no strife
The reason she's so special to me
Is because she's my daughter, you see

Her hair is blonde her eyes are blue
Her skin is fair her cares are few
She doesn't know the joy she brings
Her school tales are of happy things

A growing up young lady
She soon will be sixteen
Since her sisters have grown and gone
Tomi certainly is my youngest queen

Patricia Bramer Russell Richard

October Child

Once upon a lovely day

Came a baby with us to stay

Tiny was she on her grand entrance

Oh! What growth she's made since

Beautiful are the years we share

Each day is filled with love and care

Radiant is our lovely daughter, as she moves to each October

Pat's Poetry

Our Tom

This needs to be on paper
So you'll be sure to see
That I've just plain not let you in
On the good you've done for me

By having Tom is what I'm saying
And just so I make it clear
You have a fine son – I have a good husband
We both have a dear

From Tom, there are many things
Abundant in our home
He'll not get credit for all
But much he's done alone

There's much laughter and gaiety
And pranks played galore –
If there's foolery going on
You can count on Tom for *shor*

He has many good qualities
Here is one of the best –
A true family man rules our roost
For this, I feel we're blest

Many times 'round our table
Is a discussion live and real
We always know Our Daddy cares
He'll tell us how he feels

Not always with you, but always for you
A good husband – a good Dad
He has our respect and our love
We're grateful he's ours – this son that you had.

Patricia Bramer Russell Richard

Remembering Daddy on His Birthday

Today is my daddy's birthday
He left us and went away
The Lord wanted him for a visit
So he's gone to heaven to stay.

His hair, once red, was graying
His eyes blue as a clear day
I'm sorry he had to leave us
But God wanted it this way.

We know he's in a happy place
He's found true peace at last
In time we know we'll join him
When we, too, from this earth pass.

I know he's waiting there for us
Tho at least he's found true peace
I know one day I'll join him
When God calls my days to cease.

There will be much happy rejoicing
Such a special time to share
What a beautiful celebration
With all his loved ones there.

Special Guys

As I daydream – a grand review
Into my mind come each of you
The years come so fast to an end
Precious time with family and friend
And as there falls a fine mist
My thoughts continue to reminisce

I see four guys in my life
Each works faithful beside his wife
I count my blessings and sincerely thank
Howard, Doug, Lonnie and Steve
For being outstanding and so fine
For being kind husbands to four daughters of mine

<u>Squish – Squash</u>

They come in various sizes
And in different colors too
Lori, these little veggies are nothing
But good for you

They are planted in my garden
But they are coming up so slow
I want to share them with you
But my garden just won't grow

These veggies can be bright yellow
But I also planted green
I've searched the plants deeply
Yet no squish are to be seen

Soon they will be coming up
And it's my fondest wish
To pick a few and share with you
My delicious squish

But since I cannot find them
And my garden is bright red
Will you accept these tomatoes
And enjoy them instead?

Steve

Someone came into our life

To choose our daughter for his wife

Ever so thankful and

Very happy we are

Expecting you soon in our family

Susan Elizabeth

Someone tall and graceful
    A twinkle in her eye

Understanding and intelligent
    And just a wee bit shy

Such a busy young woman
    This crafty young lass

As she decorates her home
    With antiques from the past

Now would you dare, would you even believe
    As I watch her mature, I know much she'll achieve

Tears

What are tears and
Why are they shed
To cleanse the soul
I've heard it said

Tears are made
When the heart is hurt
They cleanse the soul
They clear the dirt

Tears come down
When my mother is sad
To see my brother in pain
Since he was a young lad

Tears fall again –
When his blue eyes filled with stress
Any you wonder why –
Yet the Savior knows best

The Master's nearby
This is His Will
God grant me acceptance
And help my heart be still

Patricia Bramer Russell Richard

The Letter

This is for that certain lady, my mama,
Who rarely gets any mail –
She's getting up in years and
She's lonesome, I can tell.

She daily makes the trek
To see what she's received –
Only to find there's nothing
To find again she's been deceived.

Although the postman's passed
And she fines her box quite filled
It's only junk or throw away –
There just isn't any yield.

It's joyful and it's a delight
It makes each of us feel better
After our trek to the mailbox
To get that special letter...

And here it is!

Thoughts to Julie in December
(Before Her June Wedding)

Christmas and our Savior's birth
A time of thanks for peace and health
A time to share our joy and wealth
A special time of love and care
And when apart our love we'll share
For beauty of the red and green
For beauty of the life we've seen

Patricia Bramer Russell Richard

To Julie on Reaching Sixteen

You're getting older dear –
But old life can be fun!
Remember, it's what you make it
And what's been done is done.

A smile can cure most anything
So always keep it with you
And don't forget to use it
As many people forget to do.

Cheerfulness is next in line –
Just try your very best
To keep those near you joyful –
This is a real test.

Happiness is contagious!
And, if happy you will be,
Your friends will want to catch it
Just so happy they can see.

Did I ever tell you
That I think you're fine?
I'm so proud God sent you
So happy that you're mine.

To Julie

Junior high days are forever gone
It's summer before grade nine
You've grown up so fast
And in such a short time

To some of us it seems
The years that lie ahead
Are often more trying
Than those we've just shed

We're always ready to help
If you ever need it
Advice will be given
You'll just have to heed it

You're really a good girl
And a pretty girl, too!
Course, I'm a little prejudice
When I speak of you

When you're much older
Looking over years back
Growing up days are funnest
And that's a plain fact

They truly are happy days
The best that you'll get
Light and carefree days
You'll never forget

There merely are a few words of wisdom
Just a few facts from an old pro
I feel you can't see any smart I have now
But as you get older my smartness will show

To Lori on Reaching Thirteen

Soon you'll be a teenager
But don't grow up fast –
When you're as old as I,
You recollect the past.

Though "Life Begins at Forty"
At least that's what they say,
Don't reach this time so quickly
Take it slowly – day by day.

Growing up can be such fun!
O, there'll be sad days, too
But life and how it's spent
Is entirely up to you.

Enjoy each little moment,
Make the most of every day
Life is so worth living –
Live it happy – keep it gay.

A "good morning" is delightful
A smile is a pleasure
Have charming disposition –
All of these can be your treasure.

Do you ever think about it?
You're our gift from God above
You are very, very special –
Our own gift of love.

To Tomi

You are a special friend of mine
I think of you as sweet and kind
Sometimes a little bit aloof
Even so at times you goof

Especially when you make me sad
No not because you're ever bad
But as you spend less time at home
I realize too soon you'll be gone

Taken away by some good looking guy
Probably Dad and I both will cry
So if sometimes I seem hard of heart
It's because I know we'll have to part

Tho I've tried to build a shell
It seems you've noticed so I must tell
My sadness almost turns to tears
As I try hard to turn back the years

Yes I've tried to dismiss my sorrow
Because I know it won't be tomorrow
But someday a ring you'll show
Then I'll know I must let you go

Patricia Bramer Russell Richard

Tomi Sue

I know a little girl
Who is twelve years old today
She's bubbly and bouncy
And has a lovely way

Only one more year before
She becomes a "teeny bopper"
But she'll always be my little girl –
There's nothing that will stop her

She rides her bike
Or goes flying in her skates
She also sits very still
With her nose in a book

Frolic and fun she enjoys
Love she brings to us each day
As we see her learn and
As we watch her play

Your Maverick, My Maverick Our Maverick

As I drove the Maverick
It seemed to be a special day
It brought back some memories
Of when I drove my Henry J

And though I enjoy a passenger
To ride with me and share
Today I counted blessings and
Thanked God for His care

But as my drive continued on
My thoughts to you did turn
I'm so glad you're happy, Julie, but
My selfish heart does yearn

For yesterday – no more to be
My thoughts ramble and they stray
For yesteryear – a bygone time
For strength today, I pray

Now as I motor down this road
I know this car has answered a prayer
The answer holds sadness because
Next to me, I see you sitting there

This, too will pass one day
This heaviness of heart
Friends we'll be – Maverick and me
As we share memories of when you were a part

Patricia Bramer Russell Richard

Fun With Pat

A Garfield Gal

I am really quite plain
And not hard to please
So just suit yourself
And do it with ease.

Garfield's a friend – in fact
My favorite pal
And he does a great job
Of pleasing this gal!

He comes in all forms –
Sizes and shapes, too!
Telephone, bank, wind chimes
And soap dispenser to mention a few.

So let's have a good time
This is nothing to fear
Having another pal besides Garfield
Makes for a great year.

Patricia Bramer Russell Richard

A Pick-Up Lady No More

I've become soft and demure
I am a pick-up lady no more
My old Ram has retired
To my spouse - for his daily tour

Now I must take it easy
No longer am I riding high
Now I must mind my manners
And drive with those who sigh and cry

As pick-up ladies who run the roads
Tho they use manners of a different kind
They tend to scare the smaller cars
And we retreat to the long slow line

I have no envy – I've had my day
Of driving a pick-up – of being a queen
Now I'll drive a Buick Le Sabre
It's the car of my dream.

A Real Charmer

It's not handsome and it's not tall
It has no personality at all
But it will soothe you and it will smooth you
It will help your circulation
You will feel the warm vibration
Won't you join the initiation
Yes, it's a real charmer
What else but a massager and foot warmer.

Patricia Bramer Russell Richard

A Riddle

I'm not "Garfield" at all
Tho I may make your mom
Want to climb the wall.

And it's true I'm not "Snoopy"
Tho I may cheer you up when
You're down and droopy.

And certainly I'm not a "Ding-a-ling"
But you may think so when
You hear my ring.

What am I?

A Set of Knees

What is a card but a message of cheer
A greeting of congrats, friendship -
Sometimes sadness and tears
I looked and I looked but I could not find
A card to identify this dear friend of mine
So this handwritten happy birthday that I impart
Is filled with every good wish from my caring heart.

And as the days fade and years disappear
Remember happy times of friends we hold so dear
Remember happy times that we did celebrate
With friends, games and good food that we ate
But if ever you're down and feeling quite low
This "Set of Knees" will start up a show!

Patricia Bramer Russell Richard

A Smokeless Cigar

This cigar is delicious
And it's great for relaxation
Just sit back and enjoy
Its wonderful sensation.

Now it is very special
Even tho you do not smoke
It's quite real, very soothing
A chocolate cigar is quite a joke!

So accept it and be jolly
In this season that's so merry
The calories are only 110
So it's not too much to carry.

A Worm Bed

I'm going to build a worm bed
Way out in my backyard
And when the birds are hungry
They'll not have to starve.

First I'll find an old tub
Made of iron to hold the slime
And start that bed of worms
So they can wiggle all the time.

And when the birds start looking
Or if they just flutter by
They can zoom in for a squirmy worm
Then fly right into the sky.

Now these birds can't be greedy
I'll put out a great big sign
That says "For Birds – They are Delicious
But They're Three Worms For a Dime"

I hope they'll not see my garden
They will see wiggle worms instead
And as soon as I have the time
I plan to build a big juicy worm bed!

Patricia Bramer Russell Richard

An Alternative

Birthdays come too often
Tho time flies by so fast
It seems yesterday I was just 16
And now that year has passed.

Now I don't mean to complain
I am grateful for each day I live
For I love life and do
Prefer it to life's al-ter-na-tive!

Chefs

You are unknown to me
But God-loving you must be
The niceties – which I do not see
Though I've heard of your sincerity.

The **C**ake – so moist and so fine
And luscious **H**am was really divine
Eggs – deviled, tasty and sublime
Fruit **S**alad – the juice like good wine.

Though other items were included
Certainly I'm not deluded
Your graciousness was not excluded
And so kind, I was quite muted.

My friend called me – she puffed and puffed
She said that meal was very good stuff
I suppose there wasn't enough
'Cause she only brought me a bite of fluff.

But you all made my friend so happy
She's begun to act quite sappy
She keeps her jaws always flapping
And I'm just disgusted with her yapping.

Dates

Don't eat all at one time

Awesome things with taste divine

The flavor lingers – like good wine

Each more nutritious and more sublime

So satisfying and so very fine.

For Bluebirds Only

This birthday greeting – all filled with wishes

And a gift that weighs up light

Is a little something that you've wanted

And now it's within your sight!

Just get out your hammer, nails and saw

And for other birds – lay down the law:

It's "For Bluebirds Only," while they have their young

If you accomplish this, your task is done

Other birds will love it, so here's the test

Just hope the bluebirds make it first to the nest

Patricia Bramer Russell Richard

Frog (In Your Throat)

Have you ever awakened
With a frog in your throat
It's just the perfect chance
To act like an old goat

There are happy people
Who are cheery every day
They take the good and bad
And with life they swing and sway

Then there are those frowny kind
Who moan and groan and fuss
This is their daily habit
To be a Gripey Gus

So if there's a frog in your throat
And you want to growl or whine
Do it only while you have the frog
To be happy is no waste of time.

Have A Whopper

Has your day been a real stopper
Or do you feel like a dancing bopper

Make a visit to a favorite point
Make sure it's the **Whopper** joint

If you wear a hat you can make a tip
And if not just swing your hip

But whichever the case may be
You'll like this most certainly

Let this make your day a topper
And enjoy a delicious **Whopper**

Patricia Bramer Russell Richard

How Old Am I?

Twenty-nine and holding is a
Phrase I've heard before
But I have passed it by
With two score plus more

We've all heard of Jack Benny
He stopped at thirty-nine
One may stop counting
But no one can stop time

Soon I will reach that special
Place I long to share
It is now becoming a reality and
We all hope to get there

I'm going to celebrate
I'm baking my own cake
Then I'll sit back, relax
And take a long, long break!

Pat's Poetry

How Old Are You?

Life begins at 40
The 50's I've been through
Now that I've reached 60
Can't wait for 62!

Hummingbird

Hummingbird Hummingbird
Where do you fly
You zoom in and out
In the blink of an eye

I wait and watch you
To take time and light
O please stop and feed
And slow down your flight

The feeder is filled
It is brilliantly red
It's crimson sweet water
Made for you to be fed

You're simply too fast
You're wings like a propeller
O won't you please rest
So I can admire you sweet feller

I've Got A Bad Germ

My doctor's tiring of me –
I've called him three days out of five
But my reasoning is quite clear to me –
I'm wondering if I'm still alive

Has someone held me by my feet
And slung me all around?
And let me go to fall and
Stomped me on the ground?

My bones are sore –
And I have some fever
A bad germ has gotten inside of me
And pulled the wrong lever.

I hurt all over myself –
Even mouth and teeth are sore
And now I even am steaming myself
And that is a really big chore!

My hair is all tossed
And filled with tangle and
I don't have the strength to
Pull on my "Wranglers!"

Drawn with pain, my complexion is pale
My eyes are filled with dismay
This body surely is wrecked with havoc
If I even cast off "Mary Kay!"

So, doctor, diagnose me and
Tell me I soon will feel better.
I'm tired of this bed and this germ
So I decided to write you this letter!

Patricia Bramer Russell Richard

Lost Keys

What was I doing and
Where was my mind
When I left my truck
With keys far behind
Hands had to be full
With purse, lunch, and fixins
'Cause I left my key
Right in the ignition

I just slammed the door
I didn't even blink
I forgot to remember
That I didn't think
Then suddenly it was five
Past time to go home
I'd worked late and
Was now left alone

Though I kept digging
And searching my purse
No keys to be found
What could be worse
I dialed my number
Frantic and fussy, angry and mad
Guess who answered - Tomi Sue
I was delighted and glad

She and Kelly brought extra keys
The day ended fine
I even did a quick change
And was at PTA on time.

Marble Slab

Have you ever felt angry, ugly, big and mad
Or have you felt sour, gloomy and so sad
If ever you feel this way
And this mood won't sway
No matter what you do
Or no matter what you say
I can tell you how to get real glad
Just take a visit to the **MARBLE SLAB**
You'll get cheered up
With cone or cup
Just walk right in and give a wave
Use their coupon and money you'll save!

Patricia Bramer Russell Richard

Nosey Hair

These little things are disturbing
They are tiny as can be
But when I peer through my trifocals
They always glare at me

Not everyone displays them
Or maybe I just don't get too close
And only seem to notice them
On those I love the most

They seem to have no preference
They decorate ladies and men
And it's alright to have them
But to keep them is a sin

And so when I am near you
And these disturbing things appear
I must curtail my actions or
I am off to get the shears

Try as I may to be nice
I only add to my woes
By worrying about the tiny things
Yes, the hair that grows from your nose!

Over What Hill?

Some say fifty is nifty
Some say fifty is fine
Then there are those who for fifty
Would not give a dime!

We've been rearing a family
We're still paying the bills
And, tho not broken down
Some are counting their ills.

But life is a pleasure
And life is a dream
If we'd just count our blessings
We'd not bust our seams.

As our waist line keeps growing
And our hair line receding
We all still thank you
And we keep on believing…

That it was just yesterday
When we had such a great start
But one thing we won't lose
Is our youngness of heart.

So, come now, and join us
You finally fit the bill
Most of us gathered are probably
Already over the hill.

Patricia Bramer Russell Richard

Pick-Up Ladies

You might say we're pick-up ladies
As high in our trucks we sit
Those who drive plain cars
See us coming – and *git*!

We motor along quite courteous
As serene and calm we steer
But drivers of plain cars see us approach
And they are filled with fear!

For pick-ups aren't lowly vehicles
Their appearance demands respect.
Ladies who drive them aren't guiding buggies
Pick-up ladies are competent and select!

Don't underestimate its driver
A pick-up lady may be large, small or frail
So you may want to move over
If you see one driving on your tail!

Pat's Poetry

Raiderette Winners

Full of mystery and good wishes
'Cause our gals kept the fans in stitches

What a cool and lovely night
Perfect for a football game
Moon was glowing – sheer delight
Oops – what a sorrow, what a shame

You say we didn't win the game
Wait a minute you left early
Too bad you missed the show
That's enough to make these gals surly

Halftime won cheers and triumph
Raiderettes kicked on to fame
Lovely gals – a great performance
Raiderettes always win their game

Silly Words

Silly words that I make rhyme
Do help me just pass the time
They pop so quickly into my head
I grab the pad and pencil lead
Some I think just don't agree
Some at times don't sound like me
But I get my kicks nonetheless
Even if my silly words don't make sense!

Speech 331 Class

He must enjoy us
This guy who is our professor
We may have other teachers
But not a better successor.

He's given us his time
He's taught us the very best
Now he's going to try us again
And we hope to pass his test.

Our class is most interesting
We've had all sorts of speeches
But then this guy motivates us
He really knows his teaching.

We'll miss our Tuesday night class
Our educational get together
We hope our final shows that
We remember speech 331 class forever.

Patricia Bramer Russell Richard

Spring Happiness

Spring is wonderful
Spring is truly great
It helps you radiate happiness
There is no place for hate
It keeps you feeling liked
Even though you know you're loved
You do not see the rain
Just the sun so high above
There is a change in seasons
Of this, we're all aware
But wouldn't it be nice to have Spring
All year round to share?

That Corner

It's nothing but junk –
That stuff you seem to favor –
It only makes me steam
While all of it you savor…

I'm anxious and mad and
My attitude is one of ire
While you keep collecting
Of which you never tire.

One day you may use or need it
That's what you always say
If I had a bit more gumption
I'd have it all hauled away!

Won't you please get rid
Of this very ugly site –
This monster may soon get me
And I will die of fright!

Patricia Bramer Russell Richard

The Nail Battle

Will you clip your toenails
I know they don't bother you
Tho often they grow so long I know
They'll curl right out your shoe

When I lie close to you
And roll over in the night
I'd like to cuddle closer but fear
Those nails might wage a fight

I'm sure it's my own hang-up and
Certain phrases coined as "tooth and nail"
Make me avoid tiny toe protectors
That are mighty as a whale

As I close these lines and I know
It happened but I can hardly see
How my neatly pedicured toe nails
Got so mighty and scratched up thee.

The Wrapping

Onto our lawn the group did creep
As silent as any mouse
And with the tissue they then began
To methodically wrap our house.

It was still and it was late
But a moon and star lit sky
Cast shadows on this funny group
As their deed was done – quite sly.

Getting even – keeping it secret
Was their short-lived, dangerous scheme
But as they quietly did their chore
Someone watched and shattered this dream.

The next morning, in its beauty
From tall, stately trees it flew
The toilet tissue did don our house
In colors of yellow, white, and blue.

Those bits of tissue still remain
As these kids near graduation
The pranks they pulled to see them thru
Was a much needed relaxation.

This beautiful class of eight-six
As senior high school days end,
Have lovely memories to hold
Of life – of teachers and of friends!

Patricia Bramer Russell Richard

Friends

A Rose from Kathryn

There's beauty in this rose
That you brought me long ago
The beauty is in you and
In the kindness that you show
And although the rose has faded
I'm returning it to you
As a token of our friendship
To which we'll both be true

Patricia Bramer Russell Richard

A Special Message

I tried to pick the perfect
Card to give to you today
But none held the "just right"
Message that I want to say.

All the verses were beautiful
And filled with lovely words
But there's a message in my heart
For you that must be heard.

And now as I write
I realize my message is clear as can be
What makes it very special
Is that it's to you from me!

A Tribute to Austin

He was a proud man
Who stood straight and tall
He left our world suddenly
And will be missed by all.

A true American – always
Showing his favoritism
He flew the United States flag
To display his patriotism.

To the nursing home
He gave a big part
In reading poetry to the aged
He was a man with a caring heart.

He was active in his church
He served his Maker often
His voice was commanding
Firm yet softened.

Some knew him many years
As for me, I knew him few
But I praise and thank my Lord
For allowing Austin to cross my path of life too.

Not always so punctual
SCAT meeting may be twenty minutes late
But we all know St. Peter
Welcomed this fine soul at God's golden gate.

Patricia Bramer Russell Richard

<u>Anniversary Greetings</u>

How many years have you been together
Does it seem like it has been forever
Have all the years been happy marital bliss
Are some of them ones you'd rather have missed
However and whatever your inclination
It's a wee bit late to change the situation!

Auntie Pat

This card is recycled
As you can plainly see
But the message that it brings is
One especially from me.

I pray you'll have a happy day
In a world so filled with strife
I ask my Master's blessing
For each moment in your life.

Not just for your own wishes
But for all you hold dear
Who want to share your friendship
And always want you near.

Baby

My heart is happy this night
For a friend who's crossed my path
My heart is joyful this night
Tis filled with glee
Tis filled with laugh.

News has come from another
A friend has found a joy supreme
She and hubby have a baby girl
Now their lives share a happy beam.

Children bind us closer together
Children really make a home
You give much love…they return more
You'll never, never be alone.

So my joys and prayers I send you three
As I ask that you receive
The happiness from yours
That my Master has allowed my children to bring me.

Beryl

To me, you're not just another
Girl behind the desk
To me, you're quite special –
It's time that I confess.

My thanks for all you've done
Some things I'll never know
In my heart, I know you're best
My girls have told me so.

Many times you've lent a busy ear
And spoken a helpful word
Love and praise and high regard
For you I've always heard.

We'll not say good-bye
Tho you'll be missed so very much
Please know that we love you
And we must keep in touch.

I just wanted you to know
My family thinks you're great
Being a friend to each one
We so appreciate.

Patricia Bramer Russell Richard

Dear Margaret

Words won't come to me today
You are so special and such a dear
When the real goodbye must come
We all will want to wipe a tear.

But this is your time of retirement
A happy, blissful one, we know
And your place will always shine
No matter what you do or where you go.

You've been so instrumental in BISD
Training children, secretaries, and principals as well
Though not directly have you trained us, but you've rubbed off
And all the Russells think you're swell!

You've given so much to education
You're an outstanding one who wants to share
Now it's time for your relaxation
But we know still, you'll always care.

You'll be in our thoughts and prayers often
And we ask, as we say good luck and good day
That you keep us also in your good wishes
Remember our times of happiness, sadness and play.

Evelyn – Did You Know?

The cookies you baked
Were so delightful
My pattern and fabric
Was simple frightful.

But – Bless you –
You came to my aid
And if I just get busy
A new dress I'll have made.

I'll make for Tomi
A pair of pants – nice and new
With those pretty scraps
I got from you.

"Seasons in the Sun"
Will be on the record player soon
Because of the favor
You did for me this noon.

You know I'm enjoying
Those Cokes – cold and yummy
They do satisfy – and
Add (inches) to the tummy.

The little desk is darling
Julie just loves her gift
And knowing you made it
Gave her heart a lift.

Your week has been full
With good deeds and such
Your friendship is treasured
I appreciate you much.

Patricia Bramer Russell Richard

Have I said "Thank You" lately
For the many things you do
And just for being you?

For Zerlina

This little letter "Z"

A thought for you from me

Is useful as a paper weight

Is given on an important date

To a friend I'll always remember

Especially in September

Happy Birthday!

Friends

Cleo's my neighbor
I know her not well
But she's a great gal
All her friends tell.

Our hearts are heavy
And we've become sad
Because she is ailing
For this we're not glad.

But God is His goodness
Warms hearts everyday
And Cleo has spirit
He's blessed her this way.

She wants to see you
She's calling you in
Her front door is open
Go see her, friend.

Glorious Fun

There are some lovely ladies
Who are special friends of mine
Sometimes they come for breakfast
We have such a grand time

They fill my day with sunshine
We talk and share such joy
One may have a new grand niece
Another a new grand boy

We're all in our middles or older
Just an ordinary bunch who
Shouldn't eat salt, eggs or sausage
But should gather for a sack lunch

Though when the eating is over
And all the cheating's done
We soothe our conscience and go back
To our diets
We've had such glorious fun!

Patricia Bramer Russell Richard

Lydia's October Birthday

For that one who collects
Spiders and dust
This web and (dust) catcher
Is a must

So I hope you'll enjoy and not take offense
For an October birthday
These things are a cinch!

One to Ten

Don't put me on a scale
That reads from one to ten
Just count me on your choice list
Of those who are your friends

Whatever is the number –
If I can ever be
A friend to share with you
Please come confide in me

But on this scale of one to ten
How do you determine rate
Is number ten high or low
And what makes number one great

Does a smile require a rating
Is warm and friendly counted, too
Are gloomy days in the charting
Tho to me, they seem so few

What's inside me won't be still
Misery shows all the way
And if it's joy and laughter
It shines through work or play

So when you are recording
Those numbers from one to ten
Put yourself right on the top
You are your own best friend.

Patricia Bramer Russell Richard

Plan a Picnic

The way you plan a picnic is
To call upon a friend
You do announce you're coming
You never just drop in

My friend's name is Nancy
She lives down in the groves
She can throw together a picnic
How she does it no one knows

But I found out her secret
She has you in mind
And she does it very well
And she's done it many times

You all get in her car
To take a tour of her town – but
She stops for that fried chicken
And that watermelon big and round

And then before you know it
You're on the Pleasure Isle
And she has all the fixins'
The personality and the smile

There's a gentle breeze blowing
And you don't need a fan
There's no need for an umbrella
Or even a flying insect can

Nancy is so pleasant
Her husband knows she's a whiz
His name is Roy Lee
I know he's glad she's his!

Polly is Retiring

I'll miss your ☺ face
No one can take your place!
My heart is full of woe
Because I'm going to miss you so.

Fun will fill your hours
I wish you sun – not showers –
I hope you have a great time
Just wanted you to know – I think you're fine!

Patricia Bramer Russell Richard

Rare Times

It's a fresh and precious moment
When my friends and I can share
The sharing times have been so often
But in the future will be rare

We never know the reasons
The when – the where – the why
But some of the sweet moments
Could bring tears to the eye

Today I'm very happy
And the Lord helps me to stay glad
And though my friends are close to me
Sometimes I feel quite sad.

<u>Reminiscing</u>

This is a brand new year and
Though the days fly by so fast
I lightly contemplate the future –
Rarely do I dwell on the past.

I visit with a former school teacher
And we rummage through some papers –
A handwriting book, a sheet of music –
Memoirs of Beaumont's early capers.

Though taken care of, I note
The condition of the pages – which
Indicates these brochures are very old
And have been through many ages.

I think now of my own life
As she shares with me, I listen
But all her words I do not hear –
My thoughts are reminiscing.

My years are way half over
As fifty plus has come and gone
And I am thankful for this new year
As I pledge to do no wrong.

As I visit now with my friend, I pray,
Like her, I keep my greatest wealth
Friends and fortune are a blessing –
But one is lost without good health.

Robbie

Robbie is a special person
My doctor's nurse and mine
She doesn't do the procedures
But deserves a ticket lots of times.

She's been speeding down the roads
And the cops she has deceived
But a smart one has caught up with her
And a ticket she has received!

Now, she thinks her day is a downer
But if she will stay in the slow lane
When she's driving
She'll be a happy and safe dame!

Something Special

"Something Special" could be the memory of a

Beautiful dream

Or a new dress sewn with a very fine seam

Maybe you like the sunshine of a nice day

Or doing just what you would like to have your own way

"Something Special" could be a

Night out on the town

Or twenty-four hours of smiles and not one frown

But this specialty will have to be sweet

Because this "Something Special" is my treat!

Steaming Low

It's always nice to talk to you
You raise my spirit high
And when the phone goes on the hook
I laugh and muse a while

Our conversation – not so important
Just the same ole chit and chat
But I smile and think about
Your mother and her hat

The stories that you mention
The water pot steaming low
And I thank your mother for
Leaving me a friend that I love so

Seasons With Pat

Patricia Bramer Russell Richard

A Loved One Lost

My friend has lost a loved one
Her Daddy kind and dear
I mourn with you today my friend
As I recall my own loss and fear.

Fear of what each day would hold
Of thoughts each day would bring
Fear of how I would control
The tears that held a sting.

But in His way and in His time
God took away my fright
And as I grew deep in His trust
Each day passed into night.

Then my Lord sent me a dream
I saw my Daddy's face again
It was a contented smiling face
No longer disfigured or filled with pain.

As I pondered about my dream
It seemed a message my God had given
To let me know my Dad was made whole
And was now with my Lord in heaven.

And though you've lost loved ones before
You still know God is grand
As each new loss makes an old wound sore
I pray God always hold you in His hand.

A Secret

I could write it very large
And tell the world – so big and wide
Or I can write it on my heart
And tuck it deep within my mind.

Change

Fall has arrived
My most choice season
My heart must warm
And not keep freezing.

Though sad and alone
My life's filled with change
I must overcome
The end of life's page.

Sometimes my heart
Fills with anger and fear
But the voice within
Tells me to listen and hear.

My dear Savior who can
Make all fears cease
As I trust in Him
I will find joy and true peace.

The Class of '53

We're gathered together
This class of fifty-three
From ole South Park High
A school where we used to be

Many are classmates who
Began school together – I think in 'forty-two
As years went by – some of us attached
Ourselves to be a part of you

Then after graduation night
We scattered to the wind
And twenty years went by
Before we met to blend

Now forty years have passed
And once again we meet
Thanks to all who are here
We each want to greet

We may have become a grandparent
Or have a grand nephew or niece
We've gained wrinkles, trifocals and pounds
And maybe even a fine hairpiece

But as we gather together
There's one thing we know we've not lost
It's that Greenie spirit within
That we plan to keep at all cost

For those no longer with us
We remember in our prayers
For those unable to come
We're sorry they could not share

We will enjoy this great weekend
From Friday "hello" til Sunday "good-bye"
One thread we all have in common
Is the Greenie spirit that doesn't die!

Don't Mourn Me Long

Should I die first and
You are left here
Don't mourn me for long
Find another "dear"

Relax and be content
Live life – be joyful and gay
The days the Lord gave us
Are to be enjoyed this way

Take your new love by the hand
Enjoy her – do things we didn't do
Laugh and kick up your heels
She will depend on you

Memories are forever
So don't mourn me long
Life is meant to be happy
So live it like a happy song

Should you go first and
Here I remain
I'll keep my lovely memories
But soon I'll be happy again…

Patricia Bramer Russell Richard

Family and Friend

The days grow more precious
As my summer comes to an end
And I recall the leisure times
I've had with family and friend

It is not in distance traveled
That I measure all the hours
For family and friends bring
My sunshine and my flowers

In my thoughts I often pass
A friend or loved one dear
But to touch and feel your hand
Is a joy to have a friend so near

Though my desk is claiming my return
And I do enjoy it much the same
It is just a pleasure to reminisce
To know with summer, you also came

So I say thanks to each of you
And I thank God for granting us this time
To smile, to laugh, to share, to love, to cry, to care
I thank my Master's blessings for my family and friend

Free Butterfly

I can soar like a butterfly
And wing into the air
Until you let me down
And then I fall right there

I am free as a butterfly
My feelings are high and light
Until you burst my bubble
And I lose all my flight

I can love as a butterfly
And spin a great cocoon
Until I feel in your life
There really is no room

My thoughts are of my butterfly
My feelings are as real as can be
But my butterfly has flown away
And I must set my feelings free.

Golden Hearts

When hearts are young
As hearts should stay
They're filled with love
And filled with play.

But as time passes
And heart grow old
They're filled with love
That's turned to gold.

Loneliness

It's my weekend –
Mother's Day, you know!
I'm alone this Saturday evening
So alone – so very low

Tom – in the poker game
Kids all away from home
Lovely weather and good health
But I'm so alone

Records on the stereo
No family for me to share
Bing sings to me
No friend for me to care

Mother's day or any day
Seems to be the same
Loneliness is all around
Is life just a game?

Lord, You gave me life
You are my true friend
Give me strength for loneliness
My life is Yours 'til end

Make-Up

Today I'm very tired
Of all this rush and hurry
I wonder why my make-up
Deals to me fast pace and flurry

I try to slow down
And ease it up a bit
But then I fall asleep
Each time I plop and sit

Lord, I'm getting older
And as shorter grow my days
There's much to accomplish
But in a tizzy I seem to stay

Down here on your earth
I try to do my very best
Guess I must wait to get to heaven
So I can get some rest

March

Magic is all around; Spring is in the air

Artists try in vain to capture nature's lovely flair

Resting winds bring soft, cool breezes

Chirping birds sing songs to please us

Harmony is so well blended in God's green earth
    – A jewel so splendid

Patricia Bramer Russell Richard

Mighty Bulldogs

It's reunion time again
A time for all our class
To have a get together
To reminisce the past

Come and gather with us
O Bulldog class of '53
No longer SAHS
But united still are we

For those who studied Latin
The language that was dead
We recall Sr. Benedict and
A class as hard as lead

United we were in religion
Catholics staunch and young
Not knowing what our lives held
Not knowing the song yet to be sung

Some of us moved on and
To other schools we went
Maybe now we feel sorrow
And share emotional repent

All our class remembers
Nettie, Adwinna, and Ed
And in our prayers we bless
Ann, Roberta, Virgil and Fred

Still filled with fun and thanks
For our class of '53
We all stay united
In our mighty Bulldog memory

My Target

Although my target date is months away
I look forward to retirement every day
To awaken and not have to dress and go
But rise and take my morning slow…
To don my clothes and walking shoes
Or to be a bit lazy if I choose
I wonder if I'll miss the present daily faces
That, with me now, must keep these paces…
Or if I'll just roll over in bed
And all job memories will disappear from my head.

My Travels

I wonder when I'm seventy
When I reach that ripe old age
Will I still be fluttering around
Visiting from cage to cage

Will I make time for travel
As some always seem to do
Or will I limit my miles
And keep my travels few

Will I keep my many friendships
To me, my friends are gold
I thank my God for all my pals
Together we'll grow old

Life seems to be a habit
Once set we seldom change
My friends have made me rich
With travels I am short ranged

But as that ripe old age I near
And all my needs are His to fill
I travel to His heart each day
And try to keep my good Lord's will

Myself

There's a ray of sunshine
Dancing down on me this day
I pray it takes the cobwebs
And washes them all away

Each little particle in its gleam
That seems to be passing by
I pray will be transformed
Into a diamond in my sky

But I know it is my outlook
And not the sunshine's ray I see
That will keep myself much brighter
And my life a happier place to be.

No Peeking

Where will I go when my usefulness is gone
When my faculties fail me and I can no longer stay alone

Today I am needed and the days hurry by
Today I am able to offer a full supply

Of loving and giving of myself to others
My acts are no different from all who are mothers

It's a spirit within – there's no dissipation –
We keep pushing and shoving with little hesitation

Though definitely I feel my body is slowing
My mind is alert and quite overflowing

With so many questions that come to me
So many thoughts that into the future I try to see

And answers I seek
But tomorrow is not mine: God does not let me peek!

Outdoors

When I'm gone
And buried deep
Don't look for me where
I've been laid to sleep

If in heaven I find
No more bliss
Than to be outdoors
And free like this

I'll ask my Master
If my spirit may roam
Outside my door
Quite near my home

To dig the earth
And turn it over
For God's outdoors is
My true love

To feel the soil
And plant the seeds
Or if I must
To pull the weeds

For on this earth
I'll have done my duty
And you'll find me
In nature's beauty.

Patricia Bramer Russell Richard

Poor Butterfly

I dreamed I was a butterfly
A flitting all about
And when I rested on your shoulder
My heart just gave a shout

And then I dreamed ridiculous
How could this really be
That I am so happy when
It's you I'm going to see

Slowly I left your shoulder
And flew off all alone
When I returned to find you
That place in time had gone

My heart is filled with sorrow
My days – empty and sad
But if I can become a butterfly
My memories will keep me glad.

<u>Retired!</u>

Rescued by age

Escaped the work cage

Time to set another stage

Important to balance life's gauge

Reveling with wisdom of sage

Enjoying my long earned wage

Decided to begin a new page

Self Esteem

Somewhere deep within us
Eternity and our aim lie very still
Left there by our tiny thoughts
Fulfilling our hopes and will.

Each new day dawning with
Some valuable goal to fulfill
Trying for that self-respect and
Encouraged as we climb that hill
Every day is a gift from God
Most dreams are reached by His love and zeal.

Slow Down World

Although I'm might near fifty-three
And feel quite well, it's true
I say, "Slow down world"
There's more I want of you

Some days are rather hectic
And these I try to shove
Right to the back of my mind
I like days filled with love

Love for my neighbor
And love for my friends
So world – just hang on
Let me grow older and just gently bend.

Spring Has Sprung

Something special happened, tho
The day is not yet here
But in the moon, the stars and sea
The message was quite clear

The saying is – you can always tell
When the birds begin to sing
But there are other ways
Sometimes we itch and sting

The butterflies also let us know
As they begin to fly about
And something in nature's world
Makes us want to laugh and shout

And tho I know it's early
There's something I must share
I know that spring has sprung
When I see a loving pair.

Thoughts on Divorce

I think of all the family
All the fun that we had
Then I think of divorce
How it makes families sad

It gets in like a monster
It tears family life apart
It ruptures all the closeness
And pulls strings of once happy hearts

Patricia Bramer Russell Richard

Waiting For Someone

I am waiting for someone
Who makes my skies beautiful and blue
I am waiting and watching for someone
I don't even know who

It's just an empty feeling
That someday you'll come along
My life will be its fullest
We'll both sing the same song

There are days that seem dim
When you come will I take a chance
Will I know that you and I
Will dance to the same dance

I try to keep my life busy
But I still long for a certain view
In many ways my life is empty
As I wait for I don't know who.

Woe Is Me

I am weary this evening
As I sit on my patio
The stillness of the day
Seems to numb my feelings of woe

I sit in the stillness
As dusk turns into night
The birds are still chirping
The tress are very quiet

I sit in the cool evening
Feeling the air of the great outside
The lights appear in neighbors' homes
In rooms both small and wide

The stillness helps me relax
Calmness embraces me
Still I am very weary
But what is to be must be

Wrinkles

The lines are getting deeper
As I get on in my years
Some are there from laughter
And others there from tears

Although they seem quite faint now
I know they'll never fade
They've made a way into my skin
And on my face they're made

I've heard some called worry lines
And some are feet of crows
When I'm sad these lines are deep
But gladness makes them glow

There are lines that cross my forehead
From eyes that lift quite high
When no word comes from my lips
But I know the reason why

I think my face will never be
One so solemn or so like stone
I'm proud of every line I have
And I've built them on my own

All these lines reflect composure
Whatever it may be
But each is special in its way
Together they make up me

Workdays

Dream On

Golly gee it's another morning
I've wakened to a new day
Must I go to work and slave
May I just be free and play?

Though I like to see friends' faces
And have a minute for a chat
Some days I'd like to goof off
Do a little of this and that.

Or just listen to a melody
I'm a dreamer, did you know
But today I can dream no more
I must get up and go (to work).

School Day Happening

You'd think it is Christmastime
But not in September
There is hustle and bustle
In the days of December

We work at a steady pace
To make this the best year
We want each day to be successful
No child must shed a tear

There are kids everywhere each
Hesitantly showing a happy face
While parents are anxious to
Get each in the proper place

There is no gift exchanging
But ever so much sharing
Each one involved is
Filled with deep caring

And tho it's not Christmastime
There's a special joy in the air
That special time - that special touch -
That special school day happening we share.

Patricia Bramer Russell Richard

Thanks Boss

From the bottom of my heart
Comes this little thanks to you
It's a warmth from inside
For the thoughtful things you do.

Like keeping me energized
With all the Snickers bars
That I find you've brought
To fill the candy jar.

And the bottles – new and old
Always are returned
For a wee bit more jelly
For which you seem to yearn.

For sharing a cup of coffee
Though sometimes it's too hot
For noticing my red eyes
And knowing when I'm shot.

All your thoughtful ways
Make my workload lighter
And because you lend a hand
My day is a bit brighter.

My Tedious Days

My work is with a computer
Not on an Apple you see,
It's the leg of an IBM –
And as dull as dull can be…

It beeps and sends me messages
I'm told they are called prompts
And I must sit quite patiently
And answer haves and have nots

If you're hyper as I am
It's such a tedious chore
At one time my work was people,
Now my work is BORE

O how I try to do it well
And try so hard to be pleasing
I paste a smile (sometimes) on my face
And hope no one notices that I am teasing.

Counselor Barbara

I have found a lovely person
Who has come to be my friend
And tho I'm not quite happy
She accepts me as I am.

She understands my feelings
And knows my needs inside
I know the Lord has sent her
To make my smile more wide.

She always brings good wishes
And tries to cheer me up
Tho I know it's far from empty
She tries to fill my cup.

So I ask Your blessings, Lord,
On this lady who's crossed my path
Give her patience and, Lord, guide her
As she tries to help me laugh.

Take away this great lump I feel
And the tears that cloud my eyes
Let me express the joy You give
Show me the sun again in Your blue skies.

Pat's Poetry

Assistant Super

I know not the exact day
Tho I know your birthday's near
"HAPPY BIRTHDAY"
Is just what you want to hear!

This greeting is being sent
With warmest thoughts of you
Not just for a happy birthday
But with thanks for nice things you do.

Like staying up late at night
And meeting hour after hour
To benefit our school district
Of which you never seem to tire.

Knowing you are a friend,
You'll listen, hear, and care
Your co-workers admire you
Your joy and sadness we want to share.

The pleasure of helping people
Is a priority in your life
You smooth the ruffled feathers
You slowly mend the strife.

And as I mentioned above
I know not the exact chapter
But a gentleman as fine as you
Deserves a "Happy Ever After."

Coach

How do you tell a body
You really hardly know
That it's been a pleasure and
That you will miss him so

Well, here is how you do it
You speak right up and say
It's been a hard year for me
But you helped make each day

It's been a joy to watch you
And hear your raspy voice
As you tell the kids how it is
The end result – their choice

They know you're on their side
Tho you do carry a big stick
The kids know you're quite fair
And able to learn all their tricks

I see you walk the halls
With your slow but steady gait
I see your career ending and
I note you can hardly wait

I'm happy you've crossed my path
Tho we never know God's reasons
I ask His blessing as you retire
I pray you have a winning season

Pat's Poetry

<u>Closing of Wilbanks</u>

I feel as tho someone has died
And it's not friend nor foe
But my beloved school building –
Wilbanks – that I love so.

As we are being scattered
Like tiny grains of sand
Not one of us must falter
We must grow taller as we stand.

We all must join in spirit and
Keep always close in heart
Memories at times may linger
But fond thoughts will never part.

So as our paths have crossed
Some will cross and pass again
And as we meet new challenges –
We also will meet new friends.

Patricia Bramer Russell Richard

Acceptance

I don't know why it happened
Or how it all came about
I just know I'm glad to be here
And so happy I could shout.

I ask for your patience
While I get into my groove
I'm quite anxious to be of service
But a little cautious and slow to move.

Some of us have worked together
We're still on a winning team
So Caldwood please accept me
I want to share your dreams.

A Bulldog Leaves the Junction

You used to read *The Bulldog*
Who surely did not bite
As his smile displayed no teeth
He certainly would not fight.

He was a friendly fellow
Filled with good news, love and fun
Now his name's been changed
And this dog's days are done.

Goodbye *Bulldog* – we enjoyed
Your news so dear
But for cowgirls and cowboys
Caldwood's junction must appear.

Continue to read the newsletter
It's filled with facts for you
Some information will be serious
There will be fun things in it too.

Publishing time is the same as usual
And it still will serve the same function
Hopefully all who read it will know
The Bulldog is now *The Junction*.

Patricia Bramer Russell Richard

Colors

Last Fridays of the month
None have a special name
They're held at Caldwood School
And they all will look the same.

They're called red, white and blue days
Peep in the schoolhouse you'll see
A bunch of cowgirls and cowboys
Who've turned just pure country.

But only in the colors of
The garments and their dress
For these young kids are learned
And great knowledge they possess.

These students have a yearning
Their curiosity is running wild
It's a pleasure for a teacher
To have such an anxious child.

Tho we proudly wear our colors
The main reason we are here
Is to continue gaining knowledge
We'll each be an outstanding peer.

Fantastically Fun Faculty Meetings

Your presence is anticipated
Your presence is required
You must come willingly and
You must be properly attired…

With happiness and a smile
With joy and good cheer
Your disposition must reflect
A wonderful Caldwood year

Everyone loves faculty meetings
They are anxiously awaited
And you can't miss this one
It is heavily slated

There will be food and fun
There will be laughter to hear
There will be thoughts of continuing
A wonderful Caldwood year.

Patricia Bramer Russell Richard

<u>A Year Goes By…</u>

Tho it's gone by quite quickly
Seems only yesterday that it begun
This year has nearly ended
Have you lost or have you won?

Did you make the most of it
Have you had a real great year
Does all your class still love you
Do you feel each child still is a dear?

Or as this school year closes
Do you breathe a stressful sigh
As you recall those several times
You could have punched Agnes in the eye?

So…what about the office
You feel it deals nothing out but trouble
Each report you sign must be
Completed on the double!

The countdown is really on us
The days remaining number nine
Let's all laugh and hug each other
This year will end just fine.

And like all the ones before it
We would have this year no other way
Lord, let us always see the sunshine
On each child's face in each new day.

Holidays With Pat

Patricia Bramer Russell Richard

Happy New Year

As I look down the lane I see
Rows of mailboxes tied with Christmas bows of red
Further down this lane I see
A new year – just ahead.

How will this new year be spent?
Will it be busy and hurry by fast?
This new year that has only been lent
Will it soon be gone, soon be passed?

Should I be ashamed for looking back
Should I be scolded for tomorrow's wonder
Today is so precious, the now and the here
Only yesterday was my new year.

Jesus is my friend today
Jesus is my friend tomorrow
Gladness and joy fill my heart
With Jesus, there is no room for sorrow.

So as I call this new year in
My thoughts are for you
Will you accept Jesus as your friend?
He's beckoning to you.

A Masquerade

The nights have become cooler
And pumpkin time is here
Soon witches, ghosts, and goblins –
Even princesses will appear.

Won't you join the masquerade?
Put your heart in the right place
Wear a lovely golden crown
Or paint "ugly" on your face.

Cross your head with an old stocking
Be an onion, old and peeled
Turn yourself into a monster or
Try imitating that sly Garfield.

Start now – use your imagination
Halloween's just around the corner
So get your act together
Come on and be a Joiner!

Patricia Bramer Russell Richard

A Thanksgiving Thought

Think about this special day

How many blessings do you count

And how many are never remembered

None are so blessed as Americans

Kindness is free to each of us

Smile – it's contagious

Give love – it's returnable

In you, there is beauty

Vitality and vigor – they fill all with joy

Interlace your hand in others

No man can live alone

God is our greatest gift

Blue Christmas Angel
(For My Girls)

This little Christmas Angel
Brings so much love to you
It's filled with joy and peace
In its crocheted thread of blue

You may hang it on your tree
In that very special place
It will reflect my love
On its wee tiny face

Just a small silhouette this angel
That has no eyes to see
But shares with you the happiness
That you have given me

Christmas Is For Family And Friend

Christmas is for family
Christmas is for friend
A time for gracious giving
A time for gifts to send
A holy, loving season
That must come to an end
We look forward to each Christmas
To family and friends

Pat's Poetry

Christmas Pace

December is so busy
No time should I waste
Although I oft' wonder if
I can keep the busy pace.

My thoughts get muddled
My spirit runs low
And then I remember
I must not slow.

Only ten days for shopping
So the sign says
Lord, please give me strength
To get through the days.

And then it arrives, the
Christmas star, bright above
Thank You, Lord Jesus,
For sending Your love.

This time of renewal
Is needed by all
Thank You, Lord Jesus
For our Savior, so small.

Christmas

God bless you this Christmas
And all the year through
Til the season rolls 'round again
Bright, shiny and new.

God keep you this Christmas
In the palm of His hand
As you praise Him in witness
Throughout the whole land.

God love you this Christmas
Sweet Jesus – full of care.
Open your heart to His love
In this season we share.

Christmastime

Christmastime comes once a year —
A special time for much good cheer
In our heart this cheer should stay.
Throughout each year, throughout each day.

We renew our Savior's birth
We recall the peace on earth
Why can we not accept the season
Every day — there is no reason!

He is our God, we must follow
His footsteps, today and tomorrow —
To have the inner peace He gives,
Our life for Him we must live.

At Christmastime, my prayer for you
Is many blessings all year through —
And His gift of love, I pray
Remains with you to share each day.

Merry Christmas!

Patricia Bramer Russell Richard

December Joy

May joy be yours – as birds fly
May peace be yours – as dry leaves drift by
May love be yours – as Christ is reborn.

Joy will not remain – the season is short
Peace is not always – it must be in the heart
Love is forever – the Savior's gift to you.

May your Christmas gift never cease –
May God grant you true joy and peace.
His love is to share – take it with you everywhere.

It Is That Season

Christmas is that certain season
Filled with festive days and good cheer
It's a time of joy and happiness
A beautiful ending for every year

It's a season to bake those goodies
You enjoy and want to share
Or give that handmade craft
You filled with love and care

The holidays are so exciting
You feel magic in the touch
Of a stranger or that special one
You love so very much

The reason is for giving
We all are young in heart
The season is for children
So from childhood never part

To sum up all of Christmas
With each message it may bring
Comes the joyous news of the birth
Of our savior and our king.

Happy, holy holidays to each of you!

Patricia Bramer Russell Richard

Our Christmas Friend

It's Christmastime again
This year has flown so fast
Let's make more beautiful memories
The kind that last and last

Let's send love to our friends
And fill their hearts with cheer
Let's give them warmest wishes
That sound out loud and clear

And though we make merry
And love our hearts may lend
We search for that inner peace
That only comes from Jesus
Our Christmas friend.

The True Reason

Merry Christmas everyone
The season's nice and new
The message is loud and happy
And meant especially for each of you.

As the years come and go
And world gets rearranged
The true meaning of Christmas
Stays always unchanged.

The store windows are brightly draped
With red, green and every hue
But in over two thousand years
The heart has not changed its view.

That it is in giving we receive
It is going that extra mile
That a sad heart may be lifted
As we share a hug or smile.

So have a joyous season
As you go your merry way
And know the true reason
Is to remember Christ's birthday.

Patricia Bramer Russell Richard

To My Family

Cheerful days

Happy ways

Rustle, bustle – loud and clear

Infectious smiles to last a year

Snowmen looking very bright

Trimming trees – what a delight

Merriment that fills the air

A yuletide season for all to share

Sadness – gladness – everywhere

Yesterday

Christmas time has come and gone
But Christmas memories linger on

Lovely thoughts of ones on earth –
Lovely thoughts of our Savior's birth

Patricia Bramer Russell Richard

Prayers

Abounding Faith

Life is a promise
Give it a try…
A gift from God
To both you and I.

We may wake up in gloom
It's our choice to make
A wonderful time of
Woes we must shake.

Both sorrow and sadness
Are hard not to see
But sunshine and happiness
This day may be.

With Jesus in our hearts
Every day is His
Our faithfulness abounds
With each promise He gives.

Patricia Bramer Russell Richard

Choosing My Path

As I begin my trek each day
I near old Walton Road
And I begin to pray, Lord...
Guide me down this bumpy lane
With lumps like a board my Mom did rub
And holes as great as a big wash tub.

Lord, this street's acquired a new look
With bordering lanes from the neighbor's yards
It's become some kind of boulevard
My eyes – downcast as I choose my path
So deep in thought and prayer
Just hold my car together, Lord, and help me to get there.

Then as I round a curve in the road
I find I'm following others – and to my surprise
Each path chosen is different – it is more smooth and wise
My route continues daily and
So the months go by - and as I drive...
I thank my Lord and say it's good to be alive.

Now you've sent your lovely springtime,
Wild flowers and green everywhere
Lord, I feel your spirit within me soaring in the air
Though I'm on the same old road
There's new life in my being
The bumps and potholes on old Walton I am no longer seeing.

So, Lord, again I pray and praise you, for
No matter where I am
Please always Lord, just continue to hold me in your hand.

Come Join Me

I am a special person
There's no one just like me
The thing that makes me so unique
Is my in-di-vid-u-al-i-ty.

When I awake each morning
If I choose to groan I may
But I always have the option
To have a very pleasing day.

Sometimes I have to sit me down
At times at me I shout:
"Cheer up! No gloom! How lucky you are
To be healthy and about."

My success is measured daily
There are two things I must do:
Love my neighbor as myself
And to myself be true.

Won't you come and join me
It's your secret – we'll never tell
Just love your neighbor as yourself
And be true to yourself as well.

Patricia Bramer Russell Richard

Contentment

It's so early in the morning
I hear the peace and the quiet
Tho I wonder why my inner self
Won't feel the tranquil site.

My burden isn't all that heavy
I should accept it as a grain of sand
I must smile through all my troubles
And be the strong person I know I am.

I've let the little fussy things
Mount inside like a puff of steam
I've lost my inner happiness
The self that radiates my glowing dream.

Of knowing I can handle anything
When in my God I place my trust
Of knowing He's the only One
Who can take care of this early fuss.

Daily Prayer

On my way to work
I say a prayer each day –
I ask my Master to guide me
In what I do and what I say.

I tell Him how I love Him
And sing praises to His name
My words are always different
But the message is the same.

There are friends who are sick
There are others who are quite well
And I ask for them His blessings
His love makes my heart swell.

Some of my friends are not happy
They have left home feeling sad
I pray to my just Master
That I may help them to feel glad
And as I thank Him for my blessings
I often wonder why
He shows me his lovely sunshine
Tho rain falls from His sky.

Patricia Bramer Russell Richard

Four Lovely Little Women

When I was but a young girl
Still growing straight and tall
I prayed a prayer to my God
On whom I often call.
It was a prayer of thought
And not a prayer of mind
But a prayer my God did answer
And blessings on me did shine.
I prayed, "Lord, when I grow older
I know the time will come
Please send me your dear children,"
He sent them one by one.
And just as I requested one day so long ago
My home was filled with laughter, love, and care
He sent four lovely little women
I know He hears all prayer.
Now the rooms are getting empty
And lonely is the hall
I find myself so restless
And on my Lord I call.
My lovely little women You lent for just a while
Are leaving home so fast,
My heart is very heavy
My face does wear a mask.
So many nights are sleepless
I find my pillow wet
You've promised peace and contentment
These days will soon be met.
I pray for acceptance
Of Your holy will
And though I'm down and lonely
My trust is in You still.
Now, about my little women
Lord and all the years I savor
I know I must return Your gift

You've lent a lovely favor
How can I ever thank You and be deserving of your blessings
Lord, your very presence even
In guiding and in sharing the young hearts
OF FOUR LOVELY LITTLE WOMEN.

Gardening

I've been an employee about all my life
And I'm weary of job stress and strife
O my God I pray to Thee
That soon you will set me free

I long to sit in my backyard
To ponder the beauty of my Lord
The yard's not fancy – just plain and neat
Mostly hard work from Charlie's feat

I beg You grant me this one wish
That soon I may enjoy wonder and bliss
And have my health so I too
Can garden with Charlie and You

Gift of Grace

I must keep your commandments
You gave me your laws
And I've broken so many
With my carnal flaws

Baptized in Jesus, given His faith
Lovingly I knew His precious joy
Then evil crept in and
I accepted Jesus' gift as a throw-away-toy

In the depths of my soul
I feel deep within
The guilt of my pain
Filled with sin after sin

With Your love, Your forgiveness
And the gift of Your grace
Someday I will dwell
In Your heavenly place

Patricia Bramer Russell Richard

God's World

God's world is beautiful
So lovely to see
The sun, the sky,
The sorrow and sadness,
The laughter and the glee
God's world is so beautiful
He made it for me.

Happy Bubble

Speak to me of something happy
Don't start conversing of the sad
The good Lord made our world beautiful
Let's do our part to keep it glad.

As we travel through life-sometimes we feel
The world is full of gloom and trouble
Push these thoughts aside and think
Please don't burst my happy bubble

So speak of goodness, faith and love
Choose to live your life
Uncluttered and carefree
My God is very close and just
And in His trust you'll find me.

Prevenient Grace

God's beautiful gift of grace
Is available in every place
We find it in all colors of race
It shines in every friend and family's face –
God's prevenient grace

The Cross on Highway 96

There's a lighted cross on a hill —
In our travel on 96 we pass it often
As we give a glance at the cross
Our hearts begin to soften

When the sun is shining brightly
The cross glows like heaven above
To show how special we all are —
Blessed by our Master's love

But if the day is foggy
If life seems down and dreary
This bright and gleaming cross
Can help us feel less weary

And when the rain is falling
The road becomes all wet
The lighting from the cross
Helps us to not fret

It's then we feel our Master
We know He's with us every day
This lighted cross is our reminder
It shows us that He is the Way

Patricia Bramer Russell Richard

Thy Will Lord

Lord, I ask for strength
I feel so low and filled with despair
Then I feel your presence
And I know that you are there

Right around the corner
You are full of hope for me
And I pray Lord
That Thy will be

Not for what I want or
For what I think is best
But I pray for acceptance Lord
Then I'll have peace and rest.

Today's Prayer

Lord I come to You today
As I often do in prayer
I see friends and many faces
Please bless all people everywhere

Let us know of Your profoundness
Let us feel You in our soul
Keep us free from all temptation
Keep our mind and body whole

As we awake to each new day
Your precious presence is all around
Let us not stray far from You
Keep us deaf to earthly sound

You have given each new life
As we strive to do our best
Lord we bring to You our burdens
Help us seek You for lasting rest

His Greatness

Blest by my Maker
These words you see
What a wonderful gift -
He gave them to me

Some have no meaning but
Most of them rhyme
These words from my Maker
I can't say they're mine

When I listen closely
As I visit with Him
His greatness to me
Is a most precious gem

Pat's Poetry

About the Author

Patricia Ray Bramer was born on December 16, 1934, in a house on Wilson Street in Beaumont, Texas. Her parents were Evelyn Anne Weyler Bramer and Raymond (Ray) Albert Bramer. Other than one year in Shively, Kentucky when she was in the 7th grade, Pat grew up in Beaumont and was the second oldest of seven siblings.

World War II was in full force during her early school days and Pat remembers the rationing of several items including gasoline, sugar and butter. She fondly remembers "coloring" the butter substitute with her siblings. The oleo margarine was bought very white but had a small yellow encased "pill" that melted when stirred into the soft fat. The children were amazed at the work of this tiny pill as they stirred the mixture.

Even though Pat only lived in Kentucky for about a year, she has affectionate memories of her Kentucky cousins (all males) who were lots of fun and good company at family gatherings. Her Uncle Vince and Aunt Mill had a pond on their property that froze in the winter and the boys would pull Pat across the pond on a sled. She loved playing outdoors with her cousins and looks back on this time of her life as a winter childhood fantasy. She also remembers the exciting times when coal was delivered; this fuel was stored in a cellar and later fed the furnace and warmed the house – Pat had never seen such a warming mechanism in Texas!

School was always a delight to Pat. She loved learning and made high marks. In the fourth grade, she showed an inclination toward music and briefly took piano lessons. Pat loved the lessons and regrets she never fully learned to master the instrument. She attended parochial school during grades 1-10 and dearly loved the nuns, especially through grade 8 at St. Anne's School. At one point in her life, Pat dreamed of becoming a nun, thinking she would love a life of solidarity.

After graduating from South Park High School, Pat took her first job as a secretary at Beaumont Iron Works, later called Alco Products. She worked in the production department. It was here that she later met Tom (Leonard Thomas Russell, Jr.) who worked in the small parts department of the company. Friendship blossomed and the young couple's courtship included drinking hot chocolate at The Pigstand Diner and spending lots of times visiting and playing games with Pat's family.

Pat and Tom married in April, 1955. The couple made their home in Beaumont and began a family. They were the proud parents of four little women: Julie Elizabeth, Amy Patricia, Lori Anne, and Tomi Sue. During this time, Tom worked for the Beaumont Postal Service and Pat worked for the Beaumont Independent School District. She started her career as the district textbook clerk in 1969; in 1977, she accepted a position as secretary of Wilbanks Elementary School. After working several years, she then worked at Vincent Middle School and finally Caldwood Elementary School before retiring from the district. Pat and Tom were married for 34 years. In 1992, Pat married Charles Richard. The couple enjoyed 17 years together; Charlie died in 2009.

Throughout her life, Pat has always treasured relationships with family and friends. Her children, grandchildren, and great-grandchildren have contributed much joy over the years. At the time of this publication, all her sisters reside in the southeast Texas area; her only brother is deceased. As the years have passed by, Pat has seen much change in her family and in her own spiritual journey. Several years ago, Pat joined a protestant denomination. The love she had for the Lord at an early age has continued to grow throughout her lifetime. Pat still considers herself a dreamer and looks forward to the time she will live with her Master and be reunited with loved ones from the past.

Made in the USA
Middletown, DE
08 January 2024